SYNCH ꞱꞁꞱꞱꞁC

www.syncholistic.co.uk

EXPLORING CONSCIOUSNESS

With Martina Grubmueller

Nina Strohmaier

CONTENTS

AN INVITATION TO THOSE WHO SEEK A BETTER
UNDERSTANDING OF WHO THEY TRULY ARE

AUTHOR'S INSIGHTS & NOTES

This is a book that has no forced structure, it has consciousness, its own aliveness. To define it is your choice.

An array of words and frequencies that fit everybody and everything at any particular moment, in any stream of time as it communicates with consciousness, in and outside of cognition. It invites and inspires the reader to step into a multidimensional space, to connect with the seen and unseen world and to develop his own knowing as he takes in and blends with the energy of the written words.

Are you ready to step outside the constraints of your conscious logical mind?

Magically free flowing, the 'story' lines evolve and re-create themselves through repetitive reading. The energy behind the words adapts and flows with the reader's molecular structure in the present moment of the now.

A meaning arises from the purity of the consciousness at that particular moment in time and space. This book is about the true empowered you, about transformation and exploring consciousness. There really is no story until you bring it to life through your focus and attention.

May the artwork assist you to ground the written words, into the here and now, and at the same time take you on a journey to your sacred source connection. My deepest gratitude goes out to the accomplished artist who took up the challenge of co-creating this book with me. Thank you, my dearest Nina!

This book is dedicated to all the magical and potent creators, the courageous seekers, consciousness explorers willing to practice sacred discipline to step into their innate wisdom, through engaging with the book in a conscious, illuminating cycle of co-creation in non-hierarchy, non-competition and non-separation.

It is my intention that it may serve as a source for more individual truths to be told, for lives to be enriched, healed and inspired, beyond this realm of known existence, and ripples of transformation and deeper connection to self to be birthed through it.

Namaste

Martina Grubmueller

1

RIDING THE WAVES OF CONSCIOUSNESS

The expression of form through a body can be measured in an instant of one moment as a simultaneous existence of past-teachings, present-creation and future-inspirations.

This complexity of this now creation requires a neutral point of observation in order to be brought to one's full comprehension.

How much of what we cannot explain bears a magnitude of possibilities before it gets defined into a little box?

Over-definition kills effortless creating and the less we try to judge the presented information, allows form to take place in its own right, filtered through the heart.

No matter how we cling to our expression through words, it is the sounds, surrounded by the light that effectively creates the vibration, taking us further into communication.

How we experience the sea of oneness is a result of how much separation we create through the walls of thoughts and feelings.

Our inner knowing, revealed through the outer manifestation, captures the colours of the true being. Nevertheless, can one confine the magnitude of this experience in a drop of tear expressed through feelings alone?

Fear stems from the mind of the future observer, conditioned into viewing life through the eye of a needle. And what if pain is the obstruction of joy by trying to fit into the narrowness of perception, misguided through millennia?

The vastness of the river exploding into thousands of tiny streams, the lack of power for authentic expression, so timidly interwoven in the accepted structures of this society.

How are we ever to acknowledge the immense potentiality of creation whilst leading humans through tiny wormholes of existence, so utterly distorted in the picture of mankind?

More and more seekers for community and sacred trust are lining the streets of ancient ceremony.

The snowballing interest for global awakening is creating ever increasing holes in the patterns of the webs, spun by the ill advised. The colours of true existence, watered down so much so, that we require fireworks to invite them back to life. Imagination calls forth a new profession in its own.

The lack of it, limits our horizons for self-creation, re-creation and out-creation of the self, a constant flow of energetic exchange between the selves living in all the worlds of existence. Turning the pages, allowing the slides to be shown, let the truth be known.

Massively enjoying the moments of unsupervised flow bursting pipes cracking concretes destructing bridges that lead to nowhere.

What does punctuation have to do with all of that? Who decides the structure of a sentence, the stringing of the letters to sounding words that make no sense?

Let's look beyond the words to understand communication, reaching above and below the streams of consciousness?

What if what we are is so excessively, exotically, impressively beyond recognition that our minds have lost the ability to find a way of expressing and comprehending?

Is this reality the dream that keeps us looping endlessly? And what if that was so required for us to finally awaken

and burst the bubble of misguided beliefs to step anew
into the vastness of this consciousness exploration?

Allow the multicolours of your physical existence to burst
open in all their magnificence, taking down the barriers
of fear, making windows into the walls of shame, lift off
the weight of guilt.

Feel the intensity of this, allow the fullness of your breath
to guide you through this undertaking. It tends to shed
some light on the simplicity of being and the shadows of
existence.

Who says this reality is not the biggest dream of dreams?

What happened to the dancing God and Goddess, the
joyful singing voices, the explorers of nature's alchemy, all
forms of healing, all forms of ancient wisdom hidden in
the darkness of the dark ages?

What depth when looking into an animal's eyes where
judgment does not exist and pure curiosity stares back at
you, a meeting of true presence almost making you
uncomfortable at first.

What is required to harness that innocence once again,
for us to be the masters of our destiny, the caretakers of
our hearts, the leaders to our desires, to see the reflections
of our own truth manifest in red roses and not guns?

Determined efforts of love labour, trying to make sense of this senselessness, creating space to employ mankind to see themselves again as healed healers, masterful teachers and co-creators of all that is.

A playground of endless possibilities, a stream of consciousness without an end, without a beginning, a sea of joyful moments looped together flowing through no-time space.

Universal time inviting you to create your own, through focused imagery in this moment of the now. It is the breath that brings it all to life, the breath of joy and exuberance lurking around the corner, hiding behind the barriers of forced evolution.

Solution has no meaning without the fabrication of a problem. Fear becomes a farce in the face of space and lightness.

The breath creates the very fabric of the moment. Breathe in deeply now, along your spine, expand your chest and pause; find your true source connection in that split space of no breath, just before you allow your breath to travel down the spine again.

WITHOUT THE BREATH THERE IS NO YOU IN THIS MOMENT OF CREATION.

READER'S INSIGHTS   NOTES

2

A TAKE ON THE MEANING OF EXISTENCE

I know that you think you know all there is to know.
Knowing is knowledge, knowledge is money!

Colourfully painted pictures, on little shiny papers, of
potent people playing with their power, so bottomlessly
drained of precious metal, source and soul.

Because knowledge is power and power is money, money
is living and living is life. So, if living is life and learning
is change, change is good. That's good. It's all becoming
clearer now, rich and poor, happy and sad!

There is no earthiness contained in all of that, but lifeless
air that keeps your feet dangling off the ground, rather
than allowing truthful manifestations to take place.

We then wonder why we wander aimlessly amongst
ghostly masked figures and figurines calling themselves
people, bodies without souls.

It is time to breathe some life into these bodies. The
exploration of senses, the spark of feelings, felt within and
throughout the fleshly mass of molecules, is no more

enough. None of that makes sense without digging deeper into who you truly are. How can you not be curious about the sourcing of this life, waiting to be explored in all its glory?

Can you say yes, perceiving the fundamental layers of innate intelligence, reaching far beyond the realm of this existence into places, spaces, times and potentials so close and yet so far?

There is no teaching until we ask for lessons to be learned. There is no river, no rain unless we seek it out to feel the urge to experience the wetness of it. There is no salty tear without the body crying it, without the one who is willing to look through different eyes into all realms of existence.

Somewhere down the line, where the line stops, is where the next line begins. The body has capacities beyond your wildest imaginations, surprising you at times, remembering long lost memories.

This innate complexity often outreaches the level of functioning in this current state of structure and affairs.

How much are we eating the food of our ancestors that has no longer any nutrition in it as we cut our ancestral connection? The money without support of precious metals, the lack of nutrients comes not only from the starving soil, but also from us losing touch with our infinite soul, that we have learned to neglect so carelessly.

Without this bigger truth there is no growth available in this existence? Have we been buying into the lies of 3D living for too long and now, standing at the edge of the precipice, getting ready to figure out the game?

Everything that we can touch, see, taste, hear, smell is only a fraction of the magic available to us.

The you, the me, the I AM, the mind, the body, the soul cannot deny itself the sacredness it truly is when working in union and communion for the greater good.

In order to investigate existence any further it requires stepping out of boxes. Standing on the shoulders of the ones before us, seeking guidance in the teachings of the past.

Meaning in itself has no meaning unless we question it through inquisitivity, unless we receive its unique perspectives, filtered through the heart's discernment, and add our own knowingness.

Until we look beyond the functions of the body, the limitations of the mind, heal our traumas and spread our wings out into dimensions of timelessness, nothing will change.

This forced illusion has allowed the puppets grow strings, being played with by their own shadows. It is time to cut the strings and stand on our own feet.

Allow your imagination to add colour to the grey and shady existence of this nothingness, to explode into the full spectrum of the rainbow being that you all are.

Go, follow the whispers of your heart leading you off piste, down the crystal cave of abundance and joy.

Restore and re-instate your heart back to all its glory and let it do its job! Allow the heat of every I AM moment bring the flesh back to life.

Observe the pores of your skin to breathe, the glands to sweat, your pheromones to call out to other worlds, calling in prosperity and ease.

Leaving no stone unturned, no mountain unclimbed, no river uncrossed to figure out what's on the other side. There is knowledge to be unearthed, knowingness to be recovered, wisdom to be remembered – what are you waiting for?

Yes, the puppets need no food, no sleep, no water, but it takes more than that to live in non-ignorance, or does it not? Who dreamt up limbs, and joints, and nerves and blood to flow in bones and veins and organs to and fro?

No box is big enough to hide when the time is up, the grand finale yet to be envisioned and revealed. It is you and me and them and us who have to make it work, to get out there, to be there and to acknowledge what already has occurred.

The free willed masters running wild, echoing the need for putting down the veil, allowing the story to end, to return home in celebratory fashion.

Call in the new beginning, nothing to fix, nothing to judge only to sacredly refocus and heal!

Neither has the mind more value than the flesh as both are just streams of light expressed into various forms.

The ever changing game of consciousness, entangling with time and space, lifetime after lifetime, taking its toll on us, leaving traces of despair and boredom.

Are you ready to leave the gambling table?

The time is now to enlist in this earthly graduation programme to claim your natural sovereign mastery, to go from student to becoming the teacher yet again?

Our earth connection is calling us forth to start ignoring the fabricated rules that stall the progress of existence. Nature, teaching master teachers to remember the known wisdom. You, as the being of the now, preparing to greet your future self in the ancient future once again.

No matter how much time it takes to find the coloured gems in oneself, don't dare to stop looking for them.

The pain, the focus, the impatience that leads up to every moment of sweet realisation is as much a part of it, as the joy and glory that awaits us in the end. Forgetting, is the process that allows remembering to feel so exquisitely fortunate.

The darkness that defines the light to bring the simple pleasures to the mind.

How many pages does a book require to be written in? What if there is no such thing as rules and measures, that requires us to shrink in our being?

Embrace the warmth of your sovereign soul that remains connected to the unseen splinters in the different worlds, in far away kingdoms.

Often the biggest storm of upheaval can help you see the light, can lead you back to choices of abundance, remember that when breaking down the barriers of incarceration.

Can you accept that invitation to the dance of multidimensional living, the song of praise for walking your own masterful path?

Start searching for the pearls of your wisdom, growing under the moss of forgetfulness, timeless whispers crackling in your inner fires of truth.

THE TRUE POWER IS IN YOU.

READER'S INSIGHTS NOTES

3

RELATE TO SELF

The boat that has set sail to look for all parts of your divine being, has sailed to many distant shores, to many sacred places of time and no time.

Now, in this time of no time now, pull in the sails, use your oars and bring in that boat to the harbour of self-inquiry.

Explore a different world of oceans, the world of inner struggle, of deeply routed dialogues that keep you in survival mode, astray from healing the traumas of the past.

Choose often, sacred over re-creation, go within and not without, let go of all shadows of destruction, release the internal doubt.

Printing the story of your adventures will have you see the gifts, the wisdom gained through all your journeys, in the seen and unseen worlds.

Allow the shells to break wide open, showing their vulnerability, their inner flesh so soft and kind. Witness this unfolding, no need for judgement to be served upon the love that has matured, so wildly tamed through all its hardship, embracing once again its softness.

Who are you?

What are you?

Where will you go from here?

Face your nakedness in the mirror of reflection, meet the God man, the Goddess woman, that kind of you that never left the shore, knowing so much more.

The sand of time reflected in their wrinkles, reborn through all eternity, never giving in, always wanting more and more and more.

Claim it now, be it now, know, perceive and receive it now. Who else, other than yourself, is there to face the wind and rain that births the sunshine without knowing. Stop asking why, stop asking how, resistance pulls you back into the ocean of ignorance and holds you captured in the ego caves.

What does it take to be that conscious co-creator of this moment in the now?

Intrinsic joy glancing over the barriers awaiting your return. Own your innate greatness, forgive the winds of polarity, forgive yourself for falling short at times and stand tall at the entrance of your sacred harbour.

Co-dependency has kept you on your sea legs far too long. Your odyssey is over, and as epic and grand it was, the best is yet to come.

Walk, hand in your own hand, defining love for your own kind, creating brand-new footsteps for your future YOU to follow.

Knowing without knowledge, feeling without touching, freedom, love, joy, bliss it all just is available to you, you being the consciousness, riding the pendulum of experience, that includes it all and judges nothing.

The burning desire to belong leads you back to your own doorstep. Ask your bones, ask your blood, ask your heart, it knows what true belonging is.

Rusty nails and creaking boards reminding us of the years of futile trying, to find happiness outside of ourselves.

The story goes, the letters change as the coloured chalk drains off the black board. There is a piece of thought!

The mourning for a long lost friend, who hands the torch of a grand purpose with awareness of its contribution, is over, as you will always be that friend to self.

Now, pick up the pieces from where you left off and finish what you started.

Do what you've come here for, as when you awaken from this dream, the world will never be the same again.

AWARENESS IS CHANGE.

READER'S INSIGHTS NOTES

4

LOVE LETTER TO THE BODY

It's been a long time coming, readily postponed, to pay you tribute in all its magnificence.

How does one begin to express the gratitude for the magic of your unique source frequency of no-time, powerfully manifested in this realm in focused form, in this now-time?

You are not who I am and yet I've chosen you to walk with me through thick and thin, to use your technology until the time is right to shed this skin.

You are the cosmic instrument of the now.

A high performance vehicle, never ceasing to impress, in constantly flowing out-creation of its daily existence. Tribute to the bones and marrow, generating blood cells by the billions, never stopping, never tiring, holding the secret key to youth and strength and magic of existence.

Access to your soul so secretly hidden in the midst of treasures, liquid gold in crimson coloured cells – permanently and eternally renewed.

Can you imagine beyond the limitations of this ego mind, where there is wisdom leading to inner knowingness yet to be discovered?

How much of what we know is borrowed from the ones who walked before us, providing guidelines, tools and streamlined skills from the past, freely dancing on the ocean waves?

Is now the time to dive into the depths of our wisdom to renew those bodies in co-creation with the secrets of the all, inside the DNA?

You are the key, what is the code, let's together take this chance to solve the mystery and finish our mission.

For the longest time I have taken you for granted, adhered to calls of paranoia of how a body needs to shine.

Reach out those arms, get on your feet, and step into that place of truthful appreciation. Open up that box of gifts that has been waiting for so long?

The rainbow colours shining brightly allowing the picture to be painted in exuberance and joy. Who is the painter of it all?

The artist of the art, that never seeks to be accomplished in just one brush stroke but never ending contributions, remains in patient awareness of the master piece to readily unfold. Nurturing is in your nature and joy is your demand.

Allowance in the making, as fraud time disappears along the way. Your brain is willing, your heart is pumping, your blood is broadcasting with no end, many rivers flowing through the veins of life lines feeding streams of consciousness, anchoring this soul into this Earth's Akashic Records.

Confusion is a daily thought that throws the spanner in the process, deviating from its original tale but not for long as grace brings back the focus to the story of truthful evolution.

Despite the windy roads, the ghastly winds, you truly find your way to source, enriched with knowing, coloured with experience, shining brightly through the eyes of man and other sort.

To always be of service, contracted out, trustingly following the meaning of the sacred lessons to become the teacher of all teachers, bridging worlds together again.

Work with me, not against me, work through me and along me, as we begin to heal thyself, this world, from its very core.

I, in this I AM presence, simply now, breath the breath of knowingness, of inner wisdom, gratitude and honour for this joyous gift of embodied life.

I LOVE AND HONOUR YOU.

READER'S INSIGHTS / NOTES

5

BRIEF ENCOUNTER IN THE PARK

As you walk through the field of green beauty in all your shine and sparkle, it is the folk of nature beings, that awakens to your light and opens up in greeting and embracing you as their own.

A buzz, a bow, a wink of appreciation that comes your way and fills your heart with tremor. A smile that brightens up your face in the ever pulsing flow of energetic bond between the you and the them.

A homecoming, a well wishing, a familiarity that so escaped your being in the past. As if the clouds have cleared, the webs have dissolved, the seeing has never been clearer than now. You nod your head, you say your words that bear no meaning to them and yet the circle is complete, no need for translation.

You leave the field much richer than you entered, a brief nourishing encounter with the brilliance of this earthly place, hidden in the midst of total silence. *TAMING POWER OF THE SMALL.*

READER'S INSIGHTS NOTES

6

A TRUTH OF YOUTH

The need for knowing, learning, becoming more, has been a never ending battle. How fond are we of flying colours, academic certifications, papers framed, papers shown to validate your being?

There seems to be a change amidst this generation, the seriousness of paper easily burned and eaten by the moths of disapproval.

It is the younger ones that now stand tall in all their tininess to show us how to think and see with different eyes of obligation.

Time to bring some light and joy into the lives of all those worriers, ease and inspired action to drive their points across.

The cards have turned, the shadows lifted, the students teaching teachers from the memories of their deeper knowing. The seedlings have become the trees of monumental change, not following the line of linearity as so often misconstrued in this reality. Stepping into colossal footsteps with their tiny shoes, small hands holding the torch of the eldership, miraculously finding fit without despair.

What is it that they know that we have long forgotten, fighting to remember in the storm of change and growth?

Little sparkly diamonds, all so meticulously cut, innocently potent, sharp and precious, just born into to this world of now.

Return to sender is not an option, as we passed the marker of no return.

Their existence has been made important to allow us to remember bit by bit, supported by their greatness, held by their loving hands in kindness, lead by their innocent embrace.

Just looking into a new born baby's eyes creates a shift of million mountains, melts open banks, rivers of ice, long frozen.

A refreshing mingling of truth and trust, of giving without asking anything in return, a way of gifting, in diapers wrapped, the present.

The crystals know them well, the animals appear to jump for joy of their return, blissful tiny powerful messengers of happiness sent to earth without a post-it note on how to handle.

The trick is not wanting to know, the task is to be curious, the wisdom comes through silent witnessing the magical transformation of the seer and the seen.

The educators become the educated, the ego turns upside down into the fountain of remembrance, the pool of divine creation to be revealed as the veil gets lifted.

The power of the small so often overlooked.

Listen to the sound of silence rather than the noise. Words will not be able to convey the meaning of this new energy alone.

So much gratitude for all their knowing, willingness to spread their frequency, little bearers of peace, proofs of multidimensional co-existence, transmitting wisdom through their, at times difficult choice of bodies, without judgment of being judged.

EMBRACE THEIR INNOCENCE.

READER'S INSIGHTS   NOTES

7

GROWING WINGS OF PERSONAL POWER

Let me take you by the hand of curiosity and lead you down the path to No-know-Land.

Walking the spirit walk, talking the spirit talk, in joyful anticipation, exploring grounds less trodden on?

Uniquely crisp the soil, fresh and unseen, not matter how far we venture into the unknown, always remember the true master right within.

Demand average to step aside, make space for renewed questions attaching to your answers.

Silver lining, insects buzzing, thunder looming, ignore all your assumptions and allow the mystery to unfold.

No fear, no thought, just trusting what arises in the very moment to be true and worth and light the follow.

No plan, no structure, no box to hide, escaping from the prison of the mind mirrors shattering, exhilarated faces as the path unfolds.

Giant leaps of letting go of what has kept you slowing down.

Do you love yourself enough to carry on?

Glowing crystals along the way, shining light on deeply seated pain screaming to be set free. Suffocating irritated voices, like old dry skin that stretches over bone, clocked up layers of frustration, just allow the rage and anger burst through the pores of self-consciousness.

How many lifetimes has it been, denied emotions, repressed tears?

You, trying to rescue others, arguing for your own limitations, innocently playing the all so toxic martyr – saver game?

Stacks of ugly words and screams of tortured bodies still holding on to being dragged along.

Say now: enough is enough, disciplined is the master, as this is now the time to let them go and find their own way of redemption.

Break with them all vows, contracts and agreements, forgive yourself, retract your energy and wish them well for we all have growing up to do.

In this moment of sacred awareness, spread those wings you didn't know you had, let the mystery unfold.

Wings of celebration and sovereign will, that carry you away from all the turmoil.

Freedom is just a choice away.

Allow yourself to spread them wide, to take your feet off the muddied grounds, and step into the safety of your own conviction.

The shining sparkle of the giant crystals, turning into a conscious stream of light, protecting you and leading the way for this journey to spiritual illumination.

Put away those crutches, no more excuses, gather up your power and wisdom, you are the one to do great work, all supported by your unseen guides and guardians, cheering for you and your graduation.

Your commitment to self, empowers your frequency, supports your spiritual wings and makes them grow much stronger.

Take this active moment to close the portals to your misery of the past, fill the gaping holes with loving heart space and turn the tears into pearls of celebration.

You have been the past, the self of the present moment, and you are the ancient future now?

The secret to true happiness lies in the exploration of who you have become on the path of this unlimited journey. Let the strength of curiosity carry you away on the wings of possibilities, feathers or not – who cares.

YOU CAN FLY.

READER'S INSIGHTS   NOTES

8

PERSPECTIVE ON THE MEDIA

Let's take a journey through the layers of propaganda, manoeuvring through the maze of passages stained with dried blood, hidden behind the walls of deception, we all bought into from the beginning as a foetus in our mothers' wombs.

Falling for our own innocent ignorance, finally now becoming more aware of the meaning for our existing selves and the paranoia ushered onto the beings of this earth.

It is high time, in this no time, to open our blind eyes and wade through the jungle of the lies and the wrongness judged into rightness?

Media, the plural form of medium, what has gone wrong? Mind readers, mind feeders, wrong fortune tellers, turn off those devices of parasitic mass fabrications in lieu of real heart based communications and make this moment sacred!

A constipated mind and gut controlling system, directing information in form of force feeds leading to serious digestive overload.

The acidity created in humanity eating its own flesh whilst contemplating what we do require in order to reach the age of enlightenment.

When did we sign the annulment papers for innate knowing, agreeing to such vile contamination of our bodies and minds?

Obscured has been our existence through the false laughter from a non-existing audience responding to pain over and again.

Here comes the manipulated story from the so called well-informed that has no reason to be heard other than causing turmoil, fear and empathic entanglement amongst the willing listeners.

It is the daily poisoning of the written word, intently printed, causing uproar secretly hidden in the black ink. No space for heart space discernment, opposing the media machine propagating war as the solution for the problems yet to be created.

Based on how much fear and disharmonious action are we buying daily news, full of misleading innuendo and untruths? Claim your sovereignty now and rid yourselves from these attacks of falseness.

Acknowledging the rightness of our innate truth and standing tall on concrete towers of this new creation.

The free-willed whispers of true source are getting louder, almost hardly now to be ignored and yet alarmingly shattered by the noise of domination, so bitterly hanging onto the powers of the past.

Control and fear have outlived generations. Industries of scandal mongering, washing each other's dirty underwear.

The notion of forgiveness, if you have it in your heart, throws anchors of allowance and redemption, of new beginnings, full of awareness and awakening.

Rebuilding faith, trust and inner wisdom in the I AM being of the moment, dumping dirty energy and washing yourself clean of all the conditioning, is the call of the day.

Free will is real and just a choice away.

A choice of choosing what has long not been an option, a thought unthinkable for many generations.

Upcycling and recycling, this is the time to use the all means of media to broadcast to the world what you are made of Hardly only blood and bones but waves of oceans, winds of change, clouds of greatness, ready to burst and be birthed again as true illuminated masters and teachers of the universes.

THE CHOICE IS YOURS.

READER'S INSIGHTS　NOTES

9

LETTING GO

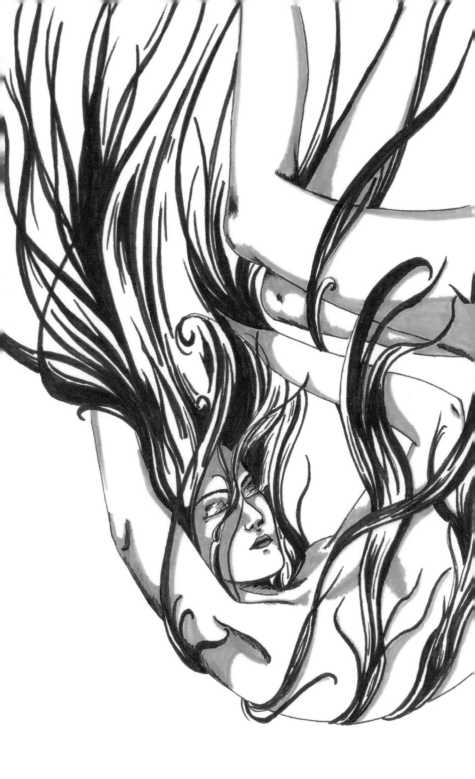

Analysis, paralysis or is the new-age desire for energy cleanliness, decluttering of dogmas and self-inquiry our ultimate heritage to be passed on to our future generations?

Sacred discipline for self-exploration, captivating not just a few in this ever growing wave of spiritual investigation, leading to greater happiness rather than to fear porn and demasculination of our potency.

The yearning for individual sovereign divinity and the focus on what is yet to come leads the way instead of self-harming thoughtforms looking to blame the culprits of the failing system.

What in the world would you rather be or do that allows you to grow and develop freely without any limitations to your existence?

Letting go of Roman numeral time, clearing programmed minds, discarding old belief systems, cleaning corners of hidden expectations and paying less attention to what does not resonate with the heart.

The grand finale lurking in the not so far distance now, birthing the new way of life and living as a result of our all co-creative doing.

What is still pulling us apart with pain, what keeps us from joining the end game? The fear of being bigger than what we can imagine often clouds the intuitive knowing, the progress, the mastery.

All your surrounding dropping hints of what you are refusing to see for self. Are you willing to be more aware?

It is you that has created all these barriers of non-receiving, and it is you that can decide to take them down.

Letting go of the cold shoulders of denial, burning bridges to no-returns, what does the colour tell you that you are wearing?

Reborn from death so many times, lost in the sea of forgetfulness, use this time of now to pay attention to who you have become.

Remembering requires forgetting, a willingness to search and find, a great deal of acknowledging what stops us in our tracks.

No matter what you fight will keep you small and take the wind beneath your sails. No more tolerance for what does not work in support of your journey.

The train of thought has left the station, your ticket still in hand you make your way to higher grounds, it's time for bilocation.

The ease of lightness carries you along the sacred power of your imagination, well out of time, well out of space. Time crumbles in your very hands as you try to make sense of it, let new flowers grow from this old illusion.

Allow the sense of pleasure being re-birthed through the tone of your own voice, the sounds of deep connection to your place of origin.

Rest your weary heads on the pillow of pregnant wisdom, listen to the whispers of your treasures within.

Be that pillow, be that rest, be that wisdom, be that treasure, be that all.

YOU ARE THE KNOWING KNOWER OF YOUR INNER TRUTH.

READER'S INSIGHTS NOTES

10

SACRED SPACE MEDITATION

You are standing on the peak of sacred mountain hearing the majestic wings of eagles soaring through the midst of clouds and rainy drops of gold and silver.

The creatures of the sky drawing into form with other beings of dragonic powers and sacred bodies of the unknown. The sky is full of them and yet there is no way of collision but harmonic circles of joy and greatness drawn into the wind.

In this magic place, surrounded by these creatures, you sense the warmth and excitement of being in the place of destiny so tenderly embraced in loving harmony of space and possibility beyond your wildest imagination.

Your voice is trembling with excitement, your feet can easily retrace the steps for your descent, whenever you are ready to leave this magic place again.

Your heart is free of weight whilst seemingly racing along the path of knowingness that this is the time you have been waiting for with all your inner pull and shivers.

There is no sun, there is no moon, in its familiar kind, and yet you seem to stand in light of never imagined beauty.

Multicoloured bodies floating all around you with such ease that bring tears to your eyes. There is no seeing as you know it, there is a knowing that you finally can see beyond the senses you have been familiar with.

It seems you are all by yourself but your body is vibrating the energy of all around you including you without a judgement, without a point of view, just pure space that allows you to be everything and everybody at the same time in the moment of now.

Your thinking has stopped and yet you wonder how your body holds this power in every fibre of its being, without exploding into the nothingness, that includes everything just now and here.

You are standing strong and tall, feeling the rocks of the mountain underneath your feet, the energy of the place is rushing through your spine and connecting through to your crown to the powerful pulsing above your head.

You are alive, alive in every cell of your being, feeling the electricity of intense presence charging through your veins and yet so grounded, sweetly embraced in the oneness of it all.

You are standing tall, in your seven colours of embodiment, lit up in all its glory, you reaching out to meet the ones long lost in all the times and places of existence, through time and no time, space and dimensions.

Everybody now is joining into the celebration, the joyful embrace of familiar colours, waves of purity and love in honour of your coming, your being, in gratitude of your long journey home.

You are exchanging presents of a kind so deeply valued changing the existence of the universe in all its glory.

Body, show me what is possible with all of that?

As it is you, bodysoul, that is allowing this experience, these illustrations and creations to be perceived, known, be and received.

Where do we go from here as this is not the end but the beginning of what has yet to come, in full creation of a multiverse of teachings, sharings, clearings, birthing of newly coloured beings.

The magic is imprinted in your body, in your DNA, in your blood, the very marrow of your bones.

Allow the frenzy of this joy be taken in to ever single cell and molecule before you make your way down this majestic mountain to sit in vulnerability and gratitude contemplating the greatness that you and your body truly be.

KEEP WALKING IN NO TIME.

READER'S INSIGHTS NOTES

11

FULLY HUMAN

If your cells had eyes and ears what would they want you to see and hear? If they could speak what would they say?

Relax, breath and call in all the colours of innate healing wisdom to saturate every fibre of your physical human being.

The intensity that you are calling pain, is signalling the end of an era, the end of tolerating the neglect of your heart based knowing as well as your forced disconnection from body and spiritual being.

How long have you been hiding in your thinking head, behind the projections and expectations of others not claiming your birth right of happy, potent, limitless being?

What does it mean to you to be fully human?

As we come to the end of time as we know it, we owe it to our bodies to seek joy and pleasure and stop the torture and neglect.

No more martyrs, no more zealots, no more being less to pleasing others, ignoring signs and signals that keep you separate from embodied humanness.

Dormant spirit, stifled needs seeking channels for blissful explosions, fully rooted in the body, in the earth.

Can you be fully embodied, orgasmically human?

Stop the excuse for mediocrity, using false pretence, lack of discipline of self as the inner wisdom retaliates in the most exquisite ways by causing pain and warlike thunders. Prepare for transformation.

Program your blood to purify, your nervous system to return to its normal function, your bones to heal and walk in unison, all so guided by the infinite source of eternal soul connection showing you the way. Your body is your pivotal focus of your current consciousness.

The sovereignty of being breaking through the walls of fear, surrounding your incarcerated soul, determined and excited to take you and your body to worlds unbeknown.

We all will be meeting at this place of new beginning soon, in all its glory, young and old, black and white, transcending colours of this world.

What strength can you build from within with a hollow spineless skeleton wandering off in all directions?

Fortify your boundaries, practice self-nurture and let your spirit hold you, let it carry you to the unknown.

Trust the power of the innate dragon, honour the speed of the eagle, for all you know they are your masterful teachers in the landscape beyond this world of war and struggle.

Sit down, relax, breathe and tend to cultivating spirit, as your body changes beyond the current appearance of physicality, your mind becomes an ally in this journey.

No matter how you define a relationship as painful, as undesirable, it is full of possibilities that can take you places, that opportunity that makes you whole and light and full of colour.

Tubes and tunnels interlinking to the system so well thought out and taken for granted throughout this time of sleep and race amnesia.

Your creative centre is awakening and leading the way back to source and innate wisdom, beyond the physical constraints of flesh and blood.

Allow the disconnect to heal, merge into the wholeness of multidimensional existence, sprouting seedlings from the fertile earth and soil connecting to the stars of brothers and sisters.

Joyfully playing in the dirt of immunity, gracefully wading through charge and polarity, cheekily showing your middle finger to the system, have some fun with being uniquely different.

Explore the breath of inspiration, reach those mountain tops of freedom, of greatness of true amazing blessings in this time of personal empowerment.

Whatever comes from that infusion, allow the graceful force guide you down the path of healing, the energy embrace your mending bodies, the skin explode in richness of the rebirth.

Old must go, new must come, there is no mustness in this process rather than the flow of what requires to be expressed through utter joy and spontaneous, in-spirited action and non-action.

Call in the sunshine, bathe in the moonlight, allow the stardust dry your skin, whilst deeply grounding the human emotion of gratitude.

Stagnant movement condemned in darker corners, shut out the wrongness that used to be that lie.

No-ness is giving you the answer for the awareness you so tightly hold dear to the secrets of the you.

The you-ness *constantly* renewing its brand, its body, its mind, its expression.

The worm that wriggles on, cut in half, re-growing its limbs, never be defeated, never allow a missing leg to stop you walk.

The eternal blueprint guiding the way in its mysteriousness, phantom re-growth of never ending stories, telling tales of long last generations surfacing again all in the now.

Flowing gently, running rivers, pebbles plastered over fields, majestic beings loosing armours being freed of jailers and jails.

ALL LIFE IS AN EXPERIMENT.

READER'S INSIGHTS NOTES

12

INNER CHILD MUSINGS

I am here and I am ready.

I journey back in time to visit my soul spark in this dimension, my inner child, who is an ascended master in an infinite amount of worlds, long time waiting for this I AM presence to acknowledge itself, to observe itself, to entangle with itself, and also to un-entangle with its other perverted selves.

I am here to listen to this inner child speaking without shutting my ears to what is being said.

The scared and teary voice of the past, I so often tried to avoid and hide from, whilst so precious and vulnerable the tone.

This child that truly does not hear the words as adults do, as her world is still made of sparks and sparkles, colours and waves of energy of sensing and feeling.

Just look in ALL her eyes, her trinity of vision, and find the frequency connection you've long lost, behind the craters of existence.

Don't let this child grow up but keep her save and nurtured, as she allows you to maintain your source connection, remembering the oneness once perceived, received as a natural gift.

Keep her fed, keep her loved until she can stand on her own two feet to walk and dance to the music of her authentic self.

Invite the four teachers: honour, trust, respect, and allowance to present unbound wisdom in all its perfection and grace.

The adventurous child being the gateway to the happy, healthy you, crossing bridges of the unseen and the unheard.

How many infinite possibilities have yet to be unearthed and opened up to all the parts of self?

This I AM presence of the now, is ready to embrace the lack of vulnerability that kept me astray from finding my sacred truth and wisdom in all this world of confusion and control.

What if the small creates the meaning to the bigger puzzle secretly overshadowed by the cries of wanting to be loved?

I am here to solve that puzzle, with the assistance of the ancestors from the past, the present and the future.

I am here to step into the role of eldership to nurture the seed of my own soul.

No more running, no more hiding, from the wanting of being understood, as I now dare to cross the multicoloured rainbow bridge to inner wisdom.

The child was in the past and it will remain so in future as there is no growing up to do.

I, who live in this world of light and darkness simultaneously, have learned to open my sacred heart to love, to care, to understand, to hug, to honour, to respect, and to protect that version of myself, who dared so victoriously to step into this wilderness of blissful existence.

I am here now for all the times you needed me, my child.

Multi layered existence ready to be tapped into, at any moment of time of need and desire.

I am the breast that feeds this I AM child in a continuous circle of finding new nurturing from the I AM adult self.

It is this child that I behold in gentle admiration that has the answers to my adult questions?

I am this heart spaced action. What you see, is this I AM, in action. The very breath that flows through my body, that constantly reminds me of 'I am not alone' helps me to forgive the self for empathically entangling for far too long.

The time is now to put my own joy and happiness as number one. The time of co-dependency is gone.

I now stand strong in this I AM presence, as a healed child and adult in my full sovereignty, in all my versions, all rainbow colours as a multidimensional co-creator, in non-competition, non-hierarchy with any part of myself or others.

CHOOSE HAPPINESS.

READER'S INSIGHTS   NOTES

13

DREAMING BODY

Well, nice to meet you finally, I AM Dreaming Body!

How come it is only now that we have been acquainted, whilst most nights are spent travelling with you from the sacral chakra?

The acknowledgement of your existence brings up questions and curious longing for knowing more about your purpose and your travels?

Who are you?

Where are you going in those times of sleep paralysis?

What are you capable of that I am only starting to allow myself to acknowledge now?

What does it take to get into the driver's seat in this journey with you, to the worlds beyond this realm and conscious knowing?

If I could just stay awake enough to catch a glimpse of what or who you are. Or is the very wish of staying conscious that keeps me in the brain instead of dropping through the throat, the heart, the gut straight into your sacred home to greet you before getting ready for dream paralysis?

A meeting of strangers and yet there is that familiar feeling of closeness, a sense of deepest honour and respect.

The I AM dreaming body's tales of distant lands and adventurous visions from all realms of existence.

With sacred discipline, upon awakening, I try to journal all impressions, thoughts and feelings, trying to make sense and find clarity within the confined makeup of my very mind.

What do you do when the dream is over? Where do you rest your tired armour from all the ventures made through times, dimensions and galaxies?

 Allow me to take care of you when you need rest and clearing of any dream experiences, imprints, frequencies that infringe on your capacities?

My curiosity keeps growing in my sacrum, pulsing cranial fluid, triggering thoughts and emotions, bringing more and more memories back to life.

The I AM dreaming body, one of the bodies most misunderstood, rarely talked about and yet so truly grand in its immeasurable experiences, reaching out through portals to the dreaming world.

Allow me to introduce myself, commune with you, inspire you, heal you from your traumas, learn from you and create new worlds together in these times of global awakening.

Let's travel in togetherness, as consciousness explorers, re-discovering the magic of the mystical realms, the places yet to be acknowledged in this ever changing tale of awareness.

Let us connect and reconnect with our tribe, all ancestors, star families, guides and guardians to dream the new dream into being.

IF YOU CAN DREAM IT, YOU CAN BE IT.

READER'S INSIGHTS NOTES

14

SAILING THROUGH THE VOID

In accordance with the ideas of others, one creates a life that does not necessarily function within the constraints of the journey to your true authentic self.

The placebo limitations found in the global narrative mind of minds grow tentacles and compute a reality, we then start dwelling in, trusting in and creating from.

You are beginning now, sooner or later, to see clearly the sea of your true potentiality.

Before you can expand beyond your current definition, you have to let go of your knowledge; knowing of the old, let go of the programmed waters of distraction and sail into the void.

The void occurs when you become aware of an aspect of your personality self that no longer fits who you are becoming and choose to pop it open, to claim it, to release it.

The meaning that you have attached to security, money, worldly possessions and this human life and death experience allows the colours to blur the vision of true happiness and inner truth.

Itchy nose and tiny toes, tip-toeing away, astray from your vast past along the path into anything that's everything.

Present moment being now, creating future selves with new dreams and new understandings of what is yet to come.

The void is a time of no time, of not-knowing – of knowing, not acting – of acting, a being and a doing in sink with the tidal waves of life and living.

A dancing stillness, a peaceful warrior grounding and mystically evolving, into a new awareness of a sentient being connected to the ocean waters of creation, trusting the wind of change and sacred discipline to power the sails of transformation.

Awareness is change.

Should awareness be change because it can? What about decisions that demand to be decided, dreams dreaming of being dreamt?

You are just feeling, you are seeing, hearing the whispers of uncertainty.

The ship has left the shore, there is no hiding anymore.

When the eye finds nothing to see, that nothingness is perceived as space, as a void. When the ear finds nothing to hear, deafness opens up a new way of sensing.

Sense the vast space as your own inner depth, pregnant with possibility, precious stillness without form, ready to explode through your authentic voice.

Allow your brain to sink into the heart and gut to think of change and transformation on how to follow the path of light and rebirth.

Essence, that which is beyond content, from beyond thought, thingness and nothingness.

Eyes, open or closed, life wants to be lived, today or tomorrow, sooner or later.

What is it you are assuming to not know to know this?

Raining drops, bad cops, hear the explosion here and feel the feelings of your new beginning, stretching cats running over bursting rivers.

You are thinking thoughts, becoming feelings, this is all there is to be, and you can or can you not?

Smell it, believe it, see it, hear it, perceive it, a new reality is behind the horizon – can you go beyond the void?

Believe it or not, maybe I am just kidding?

False passion creating energy passing through a laser, motivation sparking lazy movement, making money and all there is, is that happiness?

You are listening, you are wondering all there is to wonder. Letting go of exceeding expectations, old loves and circumstances that left you wandering aimlessly to the edge of where the old you ends and the void begins.

Constant learnings through polarity perception turning weaknesses into strengths, letting go of self-limiting constructs.

You are a perfect, yet expanding source being, enjoying the refreshing coolness of a light breeze in a world that seeks distorted perfection.

New ideas, new friends, new allies, all crammed into the body of a boat, sailing over clouds of doubters and nonbelievers, ready to explode, making magic all along, knowing all there is to know.

The time is now, the cosmic wind of change is with us.

Welcome back to a renewed connection with the universe!

Shaking hands, exchanging flowers, joyously greeting the light of a new beginning, as you step carefully, moment by moment, out the void, building bridges into new creation, dreams and inspiration.

I know that you already know these things, as you physically are extending source energy, desiring to answer the calling of your future ancestors and that is good.

Learning this or that, the new world wants you to tell of this unfolding. Tell me everything. I know that you have always known.

BUTTERFLIES HAVE WINGS.

READER'S INSIGHTS   NOTES

ARTIST'S INSIGHTS & NOTES

This is for those readers who may be interested in the meaning of the inspirational background of the drawings introducing each chapter.

Maybe you think that there was a greater thought behind these images, but I can tell you, they naturally came to mind whilst reading the written lines.

Martina has inspired me since I was a child and always encouraged me to follow the path towards my dreams.

I have to say that when my aunt first asked me to make the illustrations for the book, I initially felt like I wasn't ready for it.

After letting go of the thought of wanting them to be perfect I decided to focus on drawing images expressing my authentic touch.

The result you see are illustrations based on a naïve style which I have been practicing for some time now.

These visualisations of mine are mostly coloured in crayons, as I have loved this kind of finish since childhood.

I truly hope that the artwork supports the goal of this book, to inspire, to grow and to create.

Anin.rai.art@gmail.com

Nina Strohmaier

SYNCHOLISTIC

SYNCHRONICITIES - are more than coincidences. They are mystical quantum entanglements we draw into our awareness through the conscious exploration of our global narrative and multidimensional existence.

HOLISTIC HEALTH - is addressing this consciousness exploration of full embodiment from an entangled and unentangled observer perspective with regards to Mind, Body and Spirit.

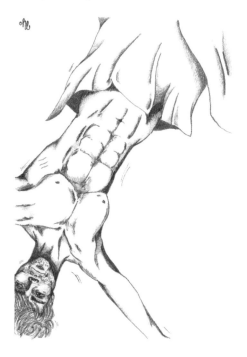

Find out more at www.syncholistic.co.uk

We are living in a placebo based reality that is rapidly changing. It is your and my manifestation of beliefs, our authentic embodied expression of celestial source connection that can create beyond the limitations of this global narrative. Are you ready to take up the mantle of responsibility of trusting the guidance of your inner knowingness? The time is now to step outside the limitations of these shared reality rules and go beyond the dogmas and deception filters of others and the world at large, through getting to know thyself. This book is very simple. It has nothing to teach you as you already know. It playfully invites you to engage the true empowered genius YOU, to let go of the old paradigm and find your unique contribution in this epic evolution of consciousness. It is dedicated to all the magical and potent creators, the courageous seekers, all curious adventurers who are willing to be fully aware of the planetary, galactic and universal changes and dedicated to practice individual spiritual hygiene and sovereign mastery. Those who are eager to step into their innate wisdom and are ready to joyously choose a different bubble of reality. May the energy of the written words have served you as a reminder of the bigger perspective, the return to simplicity of creation and allow you to embrace the infinite possibilities available to you now with ease, joy and bliss .

You have been preparing for this for a very long time.

Namaste MG   *19th of March, 2019*

Printed in Great Britain
by Amazon